Maxie Dunnam

The Wesleyan Journey

A Workbook on Salvation

Pastor Guide

Edited by Victoria A. Rebeck

Abingdon Press / Nashville

The Wesleyan Journey Pastor Guide

Copyright © 2020 Abingdon Press
All rights reserved.

No part of this work may be reproduced or transmitted in any form or by any means, electronic or mechanical, including photocopying and recording, or by any information storage or retrieval system, except as may be expressly permitted by the 1976 Copyright Act or in writing from the publisher. Requests for permission can be addressed to Permissions, The United Methodist Publishing House, 2222 Rosa L. Parks Blvd., Nashville, TN 37228-1306 or emailed to permissions@umpublishing.org.

ISBN 13: 978-1-5018-9840-2

Scripture quotations unless noted otherwise are taken from the Common English Bible, copyright 2011. Used by permission. All rights reserved.

Scripture quotations noted KJV are from The Authorized (King James) Version. Rights in the Authorized Version in the United Kingdom are vested in the Crown. Reproduced by permission of the Crown's patentee, Cambridge University Press.

CONTENTS

Introduction 5

Session One
  It's All About Salvation 13

Session Two
  For Us and for Our Salvation 18

Session Three
  Death and Life, Sin and Grace 23

Session Four
  The Blessings of Justification 28

Session Five
  Certainty with Tension 33

Session Six
  The Cross and the Indwelling Christ 37

Session Seven
  Sanctifying Grace and Holiness 41

Session Eight
  Growing On to Salvation 45

INTRODUCTION

In his book *The Wesleyan Journey: A Workbook on Salvation*, Maxie Dunnam invites readers to view the scriptural teaching on salvation through the eyes of John and Charles Wesley, the founders of Methodism. This accessible, enlightening workbook helps readers adopt for their own lives a deeper, practical understanding of salvation.

Dunnam points out in his introduction to the workbook that to be a Christian, one is ever becoming a Christian. Salvation is not only an initial decision to accept God's grace, but the continual yielding to God's work of transforming us. "Conversion—passing from death to life—may be a miracle of a moment, but the making of a saint is a process of a lifetime," he observes. The workbook, which can be used in individual and group study, provides signposts along that path.

The Study's Influence on Making Disciples

It can be easy for churches to lose sight of the importance of salvation, coming to focus instead on programs, specific ministries, or nurturing community. But returning our attention to this basic Christian doctrine, salvation, can contribute to congregational renewal. Salvation has been thought by some as a pass out of hell, which would be a static salvation that does not change the recipient. But the Wesleys understood salvation as a movement toward spiritual maturity and wholeness. Accepting salvation entails intentional effort on the part of the believer. This, the Wesleys believed, was best supported through small groups for spiritual accountability. This is not "salvation by works," but salvation for abundant life.

This group study of salvation fulfills both of these quintessential Methodist characteristics of continued spiritual development and "social religion"—that is, faith learned and supported alongside trusted fellow disciples. The Methodist movement grew because its participants worked out their own salvation as God was at work in them, to paraphrase Paul's words in Philippians 2:12-13. Today's churches can expect to be similarly blessed with transformation when committing to a dynamic, not static, salvation, revealed through learning and group support.

When Christians reclaim salvation as definitive of their relationship with God and understand it as something they live into rather than "have," they remake the very character of their congregations. They redirect their church's focus from institutional survival (motivated by anxiety) to the transformation of individuals, congregations, and communities into vessels that pour out God's love and grace (motivated by gratitude). Such churches fulfill their reason for being and thrive as ever-renewing beacons of hope and redemption for the world.

Promoting and Organizing the Study

In order to help this study have a widespread and lasting impact in your church, it is recommended that you engage the whole congregation in an eight-week study with a dedicated beginning and end point. There is power and excitement when the whole church can embark on a journey such as this together. Here are some guidelines for organizing such a churchwide emphasis.

- Select an eight-week block for the study to take place, mindful of the times that will be best for the people in your church. You might choose the beginning of fall programming, when Sunday school classes and small groups are making a fresh start, or right after the beginning of a new year in January. The desire is for the whole church to be actively invited and encouraged to participate in the study, so choose the time of year that will have the greatest impact.
- In advance of the study, plan two or three sermons on the importance of small groups, the discipline of gathering

with other Christians, and the centrality of salvation in the Christian life. With each of these sermons, issue an invitation to the whole congregation to engage in the eight-week study, announcing the beginning and ending dates.

- Incorporate advertisements about the study into your communications channels, including the weekly bulletin, the church newsletter, social media pages and posts, and signage around your church. Be sure to include the dates and times, as well as the focus of the study and a statement of what participants can expect and why it's important.
- Develop a sign-up process to secure commitments from everyone who wishes to participate. You might ask the congregation to sign up on a list, or express interest via social media, or fill out and turn in cards with contact information, or email the pastor or director of discipleship to sign up. Be sure to ask people to name the meeting times that would work best for them.
- Once you have gathered commitments and sign-ups, the pastor and staff should determine the approximate number and size of small groups, identify possible group leaders, and contact them to ask about willingness and availability to lead.
- Pastors, staff, and group leaders should work together to discern group membership, being mindful of desired meeting times and potential group dynamics. Assign leaders to groups and allow them to make contact and arrangements for group meetings, finalizing the meeting times and locations.
- Provide plenty of encouragement for group leaders, and commit to praying for group leaders and all participants as they engage in this study.
- You may choose to support the congregational emphasis through worship with an eight-week sermon series to run concurrently with the small group meetings. If so, one suggestion is to preach on the theme of "Going On to Salvation," following the broad themes and key Scriptures of the workbook.
- Finally, remember that not every church member will choose to take part in this study. That is to be expected. However, making

a church priority of participation in spiritual formation groups will demonstrate the importance of experiencing the fullness of salvation and seeking to grow in small groups.

Further helps for gauging ideal group sizes, length of sessions, and tips to share with group leaders are included below.

Leading the Group

Maxie Dunnam, president emeritus of Asbury Theological Seminary, is known as a pastor, evangelist, leader, and teacher. He brings decades of experience and scholarship to the task of helping ordinary Christians mature in faith and witness.

This Pastor Guide builds upon the directions that Dunnam provides in the workbook for enhancing the study through group conversation. The group work will be most fruitful if participants also commit to following the workbook pattern every day for the study's duration. Users will find it thought-provoking but not burdensome.

This guide offers leaders a framework for group engagement as well as ample opportunity for participants to share their own questions and wisdom with each other. The eight sessions directly correspond to the eight chapters in the workbook *The Wesleyan Journey*. Following are the session topics and goals.

- **Session One: It's All About Salvation**
  Readers will explore a number of biblical examples to discover that salvation is central to the message of the Bible as a whole.

- **Session Two: For Us and for Our Salvation**
  God's grace is available to us before we ask or know that we need it. Participants will learn how the Wesleys' theology clarifies this.

- **Session Three: Death and Life, Sin and Grace**
  Readers will confront the ways that selfishness, greed, fear, and hurtfulness diminish the image of God they bear. Yet God's love and grace are always available to those who seek redemption.

- **Session Four: The Blessings of Justification**
  Jesus came to set us free from that which enslaves us. Readers will become aware of God's kindness, which can lead them to turn back to our loving, forgiving God.

- **Session Five: Certainty with Tension**
  Participants will learn to live into the certainty of their salvation by relying on God and devoting their entire lives to the way of Christ.

- **Session Six: The Cross and the Indwelling Christ**
  God turned Jesus's suffering on the cross into the supreme revelation of love. Group members will look for the ways in which Christ dwells in them because of this redemption.

- **Session Seven: Sanctifying Grace and Holiness**
  The commands to love God and love our neighbors are indivisible. Participants will explore how being holy means not withdrawing but actively practicing this love for God and neighbor.

- **Session Eight: Growing On to Salvation**
  A process of growing into the likeness of Christ, salvation entails what the Wesleys called *sanctification*. Group members adopt disciplines that help them "grow on to salvation."

Preparation

The size of the group should be, ideally, between eight and twelve members. This allows all members to participate in the discussions. Members will learn not only from the workbook but also from the wisdom they each bring to the topics.

The optimal session length should be about ninety minutes. This allows adequate time for discussion and respects the other demands on members' time.

Each member should have a copy of the workbook and plan to start using it on the same day. You may want to give the members at least a couple of weeks to obtain the workbook. They should have their own and not borrow another's, since they will be taking notes on their personal reflections.

You may want to hold a get-acquainted gathering with group members before starting the study.

Leader Responsibilities

One person should oversee the study, to make sure the process, assignments, locations, and so on are cared for every week. This person may also moderate every session, or arrange for interested group members to take turns.

Responsibilities of the oversight leader:
- Set the meeting time and locations in advance.
- Inform members of the schedule. Perhaps send the schedule by email or provide print copies for those who do not use email.
- Remind the members to purchase in advance *The Wesleyan Journey*. They will need to complete the first week's readings and activities before the first meeting.
- Ask members to bring to each group meeting their workbook, a pen or pencil, and a Bible.
- Stay abreast of needs to change meeting locations or times, and keep participants advised.

Responsibilities of session leaders:
- Read the group session directions and determine ahead of time which discussion questions or prayers you will want to use. Try to select those you think will be most meaningful and those for which there will be adequate time.
- Prepare for the prayer time and discussion.
- Remind participants to silence their phones for the duration of the session.
- Reinforce to members that the group conversations are confidential.
- Ask members to commit to these basic principles of group courtesy: don't interrupt others; don't judge another's

viewpoint, even if you disagree; don't try to "fix" or offer unsolicited advice to another person who is struggling with a topic or life situation; and don't dominate the conversation.
- Model a style of openness, honesty, and warmth. Do not ask others to share what you are not willing to share. Usually the leader should be the first to share, especially when a discussion question asks about personal experiences.
- Moderate the discussion. Ask the discussion questions, and allow for a few moments of silence if participants wish to ponder before speaking. If necessary, end a lengthy conversation in order to make sure there is time for another discussion question that you believe is important. Remind participants of group courtesy practices when necessary.
- Encourage reticent members to participate, and gently but firmly monitor those who speak frequently or at length.
- Guide the discussion to center on personal experience rather than academic debate.
- Honor the time schedule. If it appears necessary to exceed ninety minutes, obtain consensus for continuing another twenty or thirty minutes.
- Check to be certain that the necessary materials are available and that the meeting room is arranged ahead of time.
- Bring extra pens and Bibles for those who may have neglected to bring these.
- Remind participants of the next week's session location and time.
- Ask participants to help straighten the room before leaving.

Pattern for Group Sessions

- Centering Prayer
- Bible Study
- Discussion and Sharing
- Closing Prayer and Remarks

Locations and Arrangements

- If possible, weekly meetings should be held in the homes of the participants. (Hosts or hostesses should make sure there are as few interruptions as possible, for example, from family members, telephone calls, pets, and so on). The meeting should take place in a room where conversation can be private.
- If meetings are held in a church, arrange for a comfortable, informal room.
- Participants may dress casually, to be comfortable and relaxed.
- All participants should bring a pen or pencil, their workbook, and a Bible.
- The leader should be sure that pens, pencils, and Bibles are available for those who might not have brought these.
- If refreshments are provided, they should be served after the meeting. This allows those who wish to stay longer for informal discussion to do so, while those who need to keep to a specific time schedule will be free to leave without missing the full value of the meeting time.

Not only will this study expand your group's perception of salvation, but it also will help them make "full salvation" a priority in their spiritual growth. May they be blessed by this experience.

SESSION 1
IT'S ALL ABOUT SALVATION

Session Goals

This session will equip participants to

- discover the Bible's emphasis on God's love and the human need for salvation; and
- consider their own need for salvation.

Reading Assignments

Before this session, participants should have completed the first week of reading and reflection in *The Wesleyan Journey*.

Introduction for the Leader

Group sessions will be most meaningful when they enable all of the participants to share their experiences. This guide is simply an effort to facilitate personal sharing. Therefore, do not be rigid in following the guide's suggestions. The leader, especially, should seek to be sensitive to what is happening in the participants' lives. Ideas are important; we should wrestle with new ideas as well as with ideas with which we disagree. It is important, however, that the group meeting not become a debate about ideas. The emphasis should be on the members—their experiences, feelings, and relationships with God and their neighbors.

As the group comes to the place where all can share honestly and openly what is happening in their lives, the experience will grow more meaningful. This entails sharing not only the good and positive, but also the struggles, difficulties, and challenges.

Discipline is not easy; it is deceptive to pretend it is. Growth requires effort. Encourage participants to share their questions, reservations, and "dry periods," as well as those readings and experiences they found inspiring, insightful, or encouraging. As the group members get to know each other better, they may become comfortable sharing in more depth.

Beginning the Series

This is the first time the group will meet together. Welcome participants. Introduce yourself and ask them to introduce themselves. Tell them of your interest in the topic of salvation and how to engage in it as a lifelong process. Let them know the length of each session and that sessions will move in this order: Centering Prayer; Bible Study; Discussion and Sharing; Closing Prayer and Remarks.

Centering Prayer

Invite participants to center their spirits and hearts for this time of listening for God.

Opening Prayer

> LOVING GOD, WHO GAVE US JESUS *to save us and give us new life, we ask your blessing on our daily reading and reflection and on our sharing as a group. Calm our hearts and minds so we can hear clearly from you, from the Scripture, and from each other. Send your Spirit to guide us to love and respect each other as members of the body of Christ. We pray this in the name of our Teacher and Savior, Jesus Christ. Amen.*

Scripture Reading, followed by Silent Reflection

Read aloud the following Scripture passages; then have everyone reflect silently on the reading for about thirty seconds.

- Isaiah 61:10, Luke 19:1-10, and Romans 7:15-20

Prayer for Illumination

> YOUR WORD IS A LAMP that lights our way, our God. Open our eyes to see the path you lay before us. With every step we rely on you. Amen.

Bible Study

Jesus entered Jericho and was passing through town. A man there named Zacchaeus, a ruler among tax collectors, was rich. He was trying to see who Jesus was, but, being a short man, he couldn't because of the crowd. So he ran ahead and climbed up a sycamore tree so he could see Jesus, who was about to pass that way. When Jesus came to that spot, he looked up and said, "Zacchaeus, come down at once. I must stay in your home today." So Zacchaeus came down at once, happy to welcome Jesus.

Everyone who saw this grumbled, saying, "He has gone to be the guest of a sinner."

Zacchaeus stopped and said to the Lord, "Look, Lord, I give half of my possessions to the poor. And if I have cheated anyone, I repay them four times as much."

Jesus said to him, "Today, salvation has come to this household because he too is a son of Abraham. The Human One came to seek and save the lost." (Luke 19:1-10)

Invite someone to read aloud the Zacchaeus story from Luke 19.

Discussion Questions

- Did you learn the Zacchaeus story when you were young? What do you remember about learning it then?

- Were you taught the Sunday school song about Zacchaeus (quoted in the first day's text)? (If one or more group members remember the song, invite them to sing it if they would like!)
- What lesson or lessons were taught about the Zacchaeus story when you first heard it? Did they include any teaching about salvation?
- Invite two or three members to share their favorite Bible verse or verses, and to comment on what those verses might say about salvation.
- Invite the other members to respond with what they see about salvation in those favorite verses mentioned.

Discussion and Sharing

Suggested Questions

- In the reading for this session, we learned about William Fitzgerald's four "alls" of salvation: "All people need to be saved from sin, all people may be saved from sin, all people may know they are saved from sin, and all people may be saved to the uttermost." Is this new to you? Is it a clear description of salvation? How would you explain the four "alls" to someone?
- Which of the above four have you heard about least? About which do you have questions?
- Who were the first people in your life who taught you the Bible or introduced you to the notion of salvation?

Closing Prayer and Remarks

Corporate prayer is one of the great blessings of Christian community. There is power in corporate prayer, and it is important that this dimension be included in our shared pilgrimage.

It is also important that you feel comfortable in this and that no pressure be placed on anyone to pray aloud. Silent corporate prayer may be as vital and meaningful as verbal corporate prayer. God does not need our spoken words to hear our prayers. Silence, where thinking is centered and attention is focused, may provide our deepest periods of prayer. However, those on a common journey who speak aloud their thoughts and feelings to God in the presence of their fellow pilgrims strengthen each other. Verbal prayers should be offered spontaneously as a person chooses to pray aloud; don't practice "let's go around the circle now, and each one pray."

Suggestions for a time of group prayer appear in this guide each week. The leader for the week should regard these as only suggestions. What is happening in the meeting—the mood, the needs that are expressed, the timing—should determine the direction of the group's prayer together.

Here are some possibilities for the conclusion of this first meeting:

- Think back over the sharing that has taken place during the session. What personal needs or concerns have been shared? Any participant who heard a need or concern expressed by another can speak this aloud. After each mention of a need, the leader will invite the group to pray silently for that person and/or concern.
- The leader may close the gathering with a spoken prayer or ask a member (contacted in advance) to do so.
- Thank the group for their contributions to the discussion. Remind them of the time and location of the next meeting, if that varies from week to week.
- Remind them to pray for each other in the coming week.
- If a member is hosting the group in her or his home, ask the group to thank the host. Further, encourage participants to clean up any papers, cups, or other items they may have left, and to help return the room to its original order, if that was changed for the meeting.

SESSION 2

FOR US AND FOR OUR SALVATION

Session Goals

This session will equip participants to

- consider the ways that God extends grace to us, even before we know we need it; and
- connect the Wesleyan understanding of grace to their personal experiences of God's grace.

Reading Assignments

Before this session, participants should have completed the second week of reading and reflection in *The Wesleyan Journey*.

Introduction for the Leader

Participation in a group such as this is a covenant relationship. All participants agree to uphold each other throughout the study by keeping the daily discipline of spending about thirty minutes a day on the readings and reflections, by praying for each other, by interacting respectfully during the conversation, and by maintaining confidentiality.

Remind group members that they will profit most if they keep up with the daily discipline and faithfully attend the weekly meetings. However, they need not feel guilty if they must miss a day in the workbook or have not been able to set aside the full thirty minutes for the day's reading and reflection.

If they are struggling to maintain the daily discipline, encourage them to share that with the group. In the process they may learn something about themselves. For instance, they may discover that they have unconsciously feared dealing with the content of a particular day because of what is required and what it reveals about their lives. Remind them to be patient with themselves and remain open to what God may be seeking to teach them.

Encourage them to share as openly and honestly as they can. Our growth hinges, in part, upon our group participation. Further, remind them to listen carefully to what others are saying. Sometimes, beyond the surface of the words we can sense deeper meaning if we are really attentive.

If in this honest personal sharing a member expresses a significant need or concern, it may be appropriate for the leader to ask the group to enter then into a brief period of prayer for the concern. Because the leader may miss the significance of a need or concern shared, members should feel free to ask the group to enter into special prayer when they hear an important concern raised. The prayer may be silent, or one person may wish to lead the group in prayer.

Reiterate to members that their contributions to the conversation are important. What one may consider trivial or unimportant may be just what another person needs to hear. The goal in sharing is not to be profound, but to speak the truth of our own experience.

As stated last week, the effectiveness of this group and the quality of relationships will be enhanced by a commitment to pray for each other by name each day. By now you will have written down the names of all the people in your group. Pray for each one daily, remembering what and how they have shared in the group, and what you have come to know about them and their families.

Centering Prayer

Invite participants to center their spirits and hearts for this time of listening for God.

Opening Prayer

> LOVING GOD, WHO GAVE US JESUS *to save us and give us new life, we ask your blessing on our daily reading and reflection and on our sharing as a group. Calm our hearts and minds so we can hear clearly from you, from the Scripture, and from each other. Send your Spirit to guide us to love and respect each other as members of the body of Christ. We pray this in the name of our Teacher and Savior, Jesus Christ. Amen.*

Scripture Reading, followed by Silent Reflection

Read aloud the following Scripture passages; then have everyone reflect silently on the reading for about thirty seconds.

- Psalm 25:1-6, John 6:44-45, and 1 Peter 3:8-9

Prayer for Illumination

> LET OUR WORDS AND OUR MEDITATIONS *be pleasing to you, Lord. You are our Rock and our Protector. We lean on you and draw our strength from our savior, Jesus Christ. Amen.*

Bible Study

I offer my life to you, LORD.
   My God, I trust you.
Please don't let me be put to shame!
   Don't let my enemies rejoice over me!
For that matter,

don't let anyone who hopes in you
  be put to shame;
instead, let those who are treacherous without excuse be put to shame.

Make your ways known to me, LORD;
  teach me your paths.
Lead me in your truth—teach it to me—
  because you are the God who saves me.
    I put my hope in you all day long.
LORD, remember your compassion and faithful love—
  they are forever! (Psalm 25:1-6)

Invite someone to read this passage aloud.

Discussion Questions

- What does it mean to you to offer God your life?
- What do you believe this passage says about salvation?

Discussion and Sharing

Suggested questions, based on the week's reflections:

- Which was the most meaningful material for you in this week's workbook adventure? What made it meaningful to you personally?
- Which was the most difficult day? What made it difficult?
- The leader will read aloud the first paragraph of "Reflecting and Recording" from Day Two of this week. Invite one or two members to share their experience of accepting God's gift of salvation, especially noting what was going on in their lives before they actually made their profession.
- Discuss these two truths that we considered on Day Three: one, the circumstances of life often compel us to go in a direction we never intended to go; two, sometimes we are compelled to bear a burden not our own. Encourage members to share personal experiences.

- As a transition to closing prayer, invite the group to repeat the Nicene Creed together (found on Day One).

Closing Prayer and Remarks

- Begin your time of prayer together by singing the stanzas of "Blessed Assurance" found on Day Five.
- Invite members to share their favorite ways of addressing God as they considered this in their "Reflecting and Recording" on Day Four.
- Invite a couple of members to offer spoken prayers, focusing on what has been shared by the group in the sharing time, and on the needs of the community.
- Thank the group for their contributions to the discussion. Remind them of the time and location of the next meeting, if that varies from week to week.
- Remind them to pray for each other in the coming week.
- If a member is hosting the group in her or his home, ask the group to thank the host. Further, invite participants to clean up any papers, cups, or other items they may have left, and to help return the room to its original order, if that was changed for the meeting.

SESSION 3
DEATH AND LIFE, SIN AND GRACE

Session Goals

This session will equip participants to

- confront the ways that selfishness, greed, fear, and hurtfulness separate them from God; and
- claim God's love and grace, which are always available to them.

Reading Assignments

Before this session, participants should have completed the third week of reading and reflection in *The Wesleyan Journey*.

Introduction for the Leader

Two essential ingredients of a Christian fellowship are feedback and follow-up. Feedback is necessary to keep the group dynamic working positively for all participants. Follow-up is essential to expressing Christian concern and ministry.

The leader is the one who is primarily responsible for feedback in the group. All members should be encouraged to share their feelings about how the group is functioning. Listening is critical. Listening to someone, as much as any other action, is a means of affirming that person. When we listen to another, we are saying, "You are important and I value you." It is also crucial to clarify our understanding of what the speaker has said in order that all the group members know that we really hear.

We often mishear. Asking the person who is speaking, "Are you saying _____?" is a good check question. It takes only a couple of people in a group who listen and give feedback in this fashion to set the mood for free sharing in the group.

Even though the leader holds most responsibility for follow-up, it is every member's function. If we listen to what others are saying, we will discover needs and concerns beneath the surface, situations that deserve special prayer and attention. Make notes of these as the group shares.

Follow up during the week with a telephone call, a written note of caring and encouragement, or a visit. What distinguishes a Christian fellowship is caring in action. "My, how those Christians love one another!" So follow up each week with others in the group.

Centering Prayer

Invite participants to center their spirits and hearts for this time of listening for God.

Opening Prayer

> *LOVING GOD, WHO GAVE US JESUS to save us and give us new life, we ask your blessing on our daily reading and reflection and on our sharing as a group. Calm our hearts and minds so we can hear clearly from you, from the Scripture, and from each other. Send your Spirit to guide us to love and respect each other as members of the body of Christ. We pray this in the name of our Teacher and Savior, Jesus Christ. Amen.*

Scripture Reading, followed by Silent Reflection

Read aloud the following Scripture passages; then have everyone reflect silently on the reading for about thirty seconds.

- Psalm 86:1-13 and Romans 5:1-5; 7:13, 21-25

Prayer for Illumination

> **BY YOUR TEACHINGS, LORD,** *we are warned against sin, which separates us from you and from our neighbors. By obeying your teachings, we are rewarded with reconciliation and renewal. Teach us today, our God. Give us ears to hear you and each other. Amen.*

Bible Study

At one time you were like a dead person because of the things you did wrong and your offenses against God. You used to live like people of this world. You followed the rule of a destructive spiritual power. This is the spirit of disobedience to God's will that is now at work in persons whose lives are characterized by disobedience. At one time you were like those persons. All of you used to do whatever felt good and whatever you thought you wanted so that you were children headed for punishment just like everyone else.

However, God is rich in mercy. He brought us to life with Christ while we were dead as a result of those things that we did wrong. He did this because of the great love that he has for us. You are saved by God's grace! (Ephesians 2:1-5)

Invite someone to read this passage aloud.

Discussion Question

In your "Reflecting and Recording" on Day Two, you considered the following assertions from Scripture. Look back on your notes, and discuss your reflections on these phrases:

- dead in your transgressions and sins
- gratifying the cravings of our flesh and following its desires and thoughts
- by nature deserving of wrath
- God, who is rich in mercy, made us alive with Christ

Discussion and Sharing

- Reflecting on all that you have shared in this discussion, ponder how you now think and feel about the claim made on Day Two: "But there's one thing we can't do: we can't prevent God from loving us." Do you find it easy or difficult to believe that? Tell us why that is.
- Reflect on this statement from Day Three, as you have experienced it in your salvation journey: "There is no salvation until we come to grips with the fact that sin is universal, and that it is personal, in me." (Leader, you may want to limit the responses to two or three people, for the sake of managing time.)
- Which of the following phrases describes how you have heard the message of justifying grace taught?
  » justifying us when we are utterly guilty
  » providing a sacrifice when we have nothing to offer
  » setting us free when we are powerless to break the strong tentacles of sin

Closing Prayer and Remarks

- Invite two or three people to read the portion of the "Prayer of Humble Access" they rewrote on Day One.
- Invite participants to offer brief two- or three-sentence prayers, responding specifically to needs that were shared.
- Close by praying the Lord's Prayer.
- Thank the group for their contributions to the discussion. Remind them of the time and location of the next meeting, if that varies from week to week.

- Remind them to pray for each other in the coming week.
- If a member is hosting the group in her or his home, ask the group to thank the host. Further, invite participants to clean up any papers, cups, or other items they may have left, and to help return the room to its original order, if that was changed for the meeting.

SESSION 4

THE BLESSINGS OF JUSTIFICATION

Session Goals

This session will equip participants to

- perceive how sin has enslaved them; and
- accept for themselves God's kindness, which leads them back to God's love and forgiveness.

Reading Assignments

Before this session, participants should have completed the fourth week of reading and reflection in *The Wesleyan Journey*.

Introduction for the Leader

Paul advised the Philippians to "let your conversation be as it becometh the gospel" (Philippians 1:27 KJV). Most of us have yet to see the dynamic potential of such conversation among people who intentionally practice it.

In its seventeenth-century context, the King James Version uses *conversation* for the word we would translate as *life*. Both meanings apply to our spiritual lives. We find life in communion with God and in conversation with others. Speaking and listening in a way that conveys life in communion with God is not easy. Last week we began talking about the meaning of justification. We continue that discussion this week, considering the necessity of acknowledging our sin and responding with repentance and trust. All of this is deep, very personal experience and, for most of us, not easily shared with others. Therefore, listening and responding to what we hear are very important. Listening is an act of love. When we listen with gratitude and trust in God, we surrender ourselves to the other person, saying, "I will hear what you have to say and will receive you as I receive your words." When we speak in a way that makes a difference, we speak for the sake of others, and thus we are contributing to the salvation process.

Centering Prayer

Invite participants to center their spirits and hearts for this time of listening for God.

Opening Prayer

> LOVING GOD, WHO GAVE US JESUS *to save us and give us new life, we ask your blessing on our daily reading and reflection and on our sharing as a group. Calm our hearts and minds so we can hear clearly from you, from the Scripture, and from each other. Send your Spirit to guide us to love and respect each other as members of the body of Christ. We pray this in the name of our Teacher and Savior, Jesus Christ. Amen.*

Scripture Reading, followed by Silent Reflection

Read aloud the following Scripture passages; then have everyone reflect silently on the reading for about thirty seconds.

- Psalm 32:1-2, Mark 1:14-15, and Romans 14:9-12

| *Prayer for Illumination* | **WE HUMBLY RECEIVE** *the gift that there is no condemnation for those who are in Christ Jesus. Draw us to you and make our listening and speaking worthy of a disciple of Jesus. Amen.* |

Bible Study

He rescued us from the control of darkness and transferred us into the kingdom of the Son he loves. He set us free through the Son and forgave our sins. (Colossians 1:13-14)

Invite someone to read this passage aloud.

Discussion question

- In what ways do the words *rescued* and *transferred* describe the work of salvation?

Discussion and Sharing

- We learned from Paul's letter to the Romans that God's kindness leads us to repentance. There are two requirements for genuine repentance. One is remedial: that we turn around and seek an entirely new personal orientation. The other is positive: that we believe the good news that Jesus comes to offer. How do you see these working in your life?
- On Day Two, you were asked to find an occasion to talk to someone about repentance, asking for their thoughts and sharing the observations from our study. Leader, invite a couple of participants to talk about their experience of this sharing.
- On Day Two, members wrote prayers of repentance and believing. Leader, invite a couple of group members to read the prayers they wrote. Ask the other members to listen in love and ask questions in conversation that "becometh the gospel."

- Invite a group member to read aloud the last paragraph of Day Three's commentary. Ask the group: How we are we justified by grace through believing?
- Discuss the idea of judgment: the fact of it, how we seek to evade it, how the fact of judgment should influence our sharing of the gospel with others.

Closing Prayer and Remarks

Corporate prayer is one of the great blessings of Christian community. To affirm that is one thing; to experience it is another. To experience it we have to experiment with it.

- Spend three to five minutes in quiet, reflecting on your salvation journey. Where are you on that journey? In what you have read and discussed in the group, what has raised questions for you? What may be missing in your repenting and believing for justification?
- Let each person who wishes to do so share one need he or she has identified in the time of silent reflection. All listen quietly and prayerfully, without comment, until as many as will have shared. The leader and others may want to take notes, for follow-up prayer.
- There is a sense in which, through this sharing, you have been praying. There is power in a community of people on a common journey who verbalize their thoughts and feelings to God in the presence of fellow pilgrims. Invite members to pray aloud in this closing time. They should offer brief prayers for other members, making sure that all who expressed a need have been mentioned.
- If the group is meeting in a place where this would not be disruptive to others, end the time by singing the first stanza of "Amazing Grace."
- Thank the group for their contributions to the discussion. Remind them of the time and location of the next meeting, if that varies from week to week.

- Remind them to pray for each other in the coming week.
- If a member is hosting the group in her or his home, ask the group to thank the host. Further, invite participants to clean up any papers, cups, or other items they may have left, and to help return the room to its original order, if that was changed for the meeting.

SESSION 5

CERTAINTY WITH TENSION

Session Goals

This session will equip participants to
- live into the certainty of their salvation by relying on God; and
- practice devoting themselves thoroughly to the way of Christ.

Reading Assignments

Before this session, participants should have completed the fifth week of reading and reflection in *The Wesleyan Journey*.

Introduction for the Leader

Though we can live in confidence because of our life in Christ, there is often tension even with our certainty. Just as that is true in our own Christian life, it is an issue in groups. Group members often disagree, and emotions are always involved when we are sharing deep convictions. Hopefully, you have cultivated trust in this group, enabling them to share honestly. In our sharing we always run the risk of being misunderstood, but our commitment to Christian conferencing should free us to risk. The way we listen and respond will free our fellow pilgrims to be willing to risk sharing.

Take the time needed to ensure clarity. When participants disagree, ask them to check to determine whether they have heard accurately. Encourage them to ask questions. Even though one member may disagree vehemently with another, they need not express that immediately.

Centering Prayer

Invite participants to center their spirits and hearts for this time of listening for God.

Opening Prayer

> LOVING GOD, WHO GAVE US JESUS *to save us and give us new life, we ask your blessing on our daily reading and reflection and on our sharing as a group. Calm our hearts and minds so we can hear clearly from you, from the Scripture, and from each other. Send your Spirit to guide us to love and respect each other as members of the body of Christ. We pray this in the name of our Teacher and Savior, Jesus Christ. Amen.*

Scripture Reading, followed by Silent Reflection

Read aloud the following Scripture passages; then have everyone reflect silently on the reading for about thirty seconds.

- Psalm 103:1-12, Luke 6:32-36, and Romans 8:1-17

Prayer for Illumination

> JESUS, WE THANK YOU *for your sacrifice to redeem us. May we express our grateful faith by sacrificing for others, that they too may seek and find new life in you. Amen.*

Hymn

Sing the stanza of "Blessed Assurance" found on Day Three.

Bible Study

My brothers and sisters, what good is it if people say they have faith but do nothing to show it? Claiming to have faith can't save anyone, can it? Imagine a brother or sister who is naked and never has enough food to eat. What if one of you said, "Go in peace! Stay warm! Have a nice meal!"? What good is it if you don't actually give them what their body needs? In the same way, faith is dead when it doesn't result in faithful activity.

Someone might claim, "You have faith and I have action." But how can I see your faith apart from your actions? Instead, I'll show you my faith by putting it into practice in faithful action.

(James 2:14-18)

Invite someone to read this passage aloud.

Discussion question

The letter from James asserts that both faith and works are part of salvation. Do you believe that faith in the redeeming sacrifice of Jesus is all that is needed for salvation? What do you think of the claim that we are mocking the gospel if we reduce its requirements to simply giving intellectual assent to Jesus's sacrifice and accept by faith the eternal security he offers?

Discussion and Sharing

- Spend ten to fifteen minutes talking about sin in the life of the believer. Is it possible to lose one's salvation? Look back on your reflections on Days One and Two.
- What do you think about the claim that whether we *can* or *can't* fall is not as important as whether we *do* or *don't* fall?
- Invite two or three participants to share their experience of assurance.
- Invite two or three participants to share how on Day Four they put Charles Wesley's hymn "Where Shall My Wondering Soul Begin" in their own words.

- Thinking about what has been shared by your fellow pilgrims, do you think assurance helps us in our life and witness? In what ways?
- Spend the time remaining asking members what they think about the following assertions:
  » We can't claim Jesus as Savior without a willingness to surrender to him as Lord.
  » An emphasis on faith that does not include fidelity to Christ's call to walk in newness of life is a distortion of the gospel.
  » A faith that emphasizes ethics and good works as a way to earn salvation is a false faith. Ethics and good works do not save us, but rather are the expression of the transforming work of the Spirit within us.

Closing Prayer and Remarks

- Spontaneous conversational prayer is a creative source in our corporate life. Close your time together by inviting as many as will to offer brief prayers, particularly for thoughts and concerns that members have shared in this session. Before you begin praying, ask if anyone in the group has specific prayer requests. When as many as wish have prayed, close by inviting all to pray together the Lord's Prayer.
- Thank the group for their contributions to the discussion. Remind them of the time and location of the next meeting, if that varies from week to week.
- Remind them to pray for each other in the coming week.
- If a member is hosting the group in her or his home, ask the group to thank the host. Further, invite participants to clean up any papers, cups, or other items they may have left, and to help return the room to its original order, if that was changed for the meeting.

SESSION 6

THE CROSS AND THE INDWELLING CHRIST

Session Goals

This session will equip participants to

- perceive how God turned Jesus's suffering on the cross into the supreme revelation of love; and
- allow Christ to dwell in them and shape their lives.

Reading Assignments

Before this session, participants should have completed the sixth week of reading and reflection in *The Wesleyan Journey*.

Introduction for the Leader

You are nearing the close of this workbook adventure. After this session, there will be only two remaining planned group meetings.

This would be a good time to ask the group members if they are interested in continuing to meet together after this study ends and use a different shared resource.

Centering Prayer

Invite participants to center their spirits and hearts for this time of listening for God.

Opening Prayer

> LOVING GOD, WHO GAVE US JESUS *to save us and give us new life, we ask your blessing on our daily reading and reflection and on our sharing as a group. Calm our hearts and minds so we can hear clearly from you, from the Scripture, and from each other. Send your Spirit to guide us to love and respect each other as members of the body of Christ. We pray this in the name of our Teacher and Savior, Jesus Christ. Amen.*

Scripture Reading, followed by Silent Reflection

Read aloud the following Scripture passages; then have everyone reflect silently on the reading for about thirty seconds.

- Psalm 51:1-10, 2 Corinthians 5:17, and Galatians 2:17-20

Prayer for Illumination

> GOD, GRANT US *awareness of the indwelling Christ and to yield to his power to shape our lives. Amen.*

Hymn

Sing the first stanza and chorus of "Alas! and Did My Savior Bleed" (often remembered as "At the Cross") found on Day One.

Bible Study

I have been crucified with Christ and I no longer live, but Christ lives in me. (Galatians 2:20a)

Invite someone to read this passage aloud.

Discussion questions

- What do you think it means to be "crucified with Christ"?
- Did you memorize and repeat to yourself the verse, "I no longer live, but Christ lives in me"?
- What was that like for you?
- What does it mean to have "union with Christ"? Is this ever a part of your spiritual life?

Discussion and Sharing

- Invite two or three members to share what they wrote in their "Reflecting and Recording" on Day One.
- The theme of Day Three is "Love and Sacrifice Go Together." Invite two or three members to share their personal experience of sacrificial love that they recorded that day. Ask the group, How might those experiences reflect the way that Jesus's death on the cross is the ultimate picture of how love and sacrifice go together?
- Spend the balance of your time discussing how the shaping power of the indwelling Christ works in your life. Share personal experiences.

Closing Prayer and Remarks

- Invite the group to sing again the stanza and chorus of "Alas! and Did My Savior Bleed" ("At the Cross") found on Day One.
- Ask members if any believe that they are having to make some level of sacrifice out of love for someone. If they did not share in the earlier discussion, invite them to do so now.
- Then lead the group in corporate prayer, making sure each person who has spoken about making a sacrifice is mentioned.
- Invite members to share any concern or need for which they would like prayer. Again, after sharing, lead the group in corporate prayer, making sure each expressed need is mentioned.

- After concluding the prayer, ask the participants to bless one another with this benediction from Numbers 6:24-26:

The Lord bless you and protect you.
The Lord make his face shine on you and be gracious to you.
The Lord lift up his face to you and grant you peace.

- Thank the group for their contributions to the discussion. Remind them of the time and location of the next meeting, if that varies from week to week.
- Remind them to pray for each other in the coming week.
- If a member is hosting the group in her or his home, ask the group to thank the host. Further, invite participants to clean up any papers, cups, or other items they may have left, and to help return the room to its original order, if that was changed for the meeting.

SESSION 7
SANCTIFYING GRACE AND HOLINESS

Session Goals

This session will equip participants to

- learn what it means to "be holy"; and
- discern how they might practice holiness in their lives.

Reading Assignments

Before this session, participants should have completed the seventh week of reading and reflection in *The Wesleyan Journey*.

Introduction for the Leader

During the previous session, the group may have discussed the possibility of continuing to meet for study and discussion. Here are some options the group might consider:

- Select two or three weeks of this workbook that were especially difficult or meaningful and revisit them for an additional two or three weeks.
- Gather again as a group and use another study resource. Ask two or three members to bring resource suggestions to the

group next week. They may find some options at cokesbury.com.
- If the group appreciates this workbook approach to reading and reflection, they may be interested in other, similar workbooks by Maxie Dunnam:
  » *The Workbook of Living Prayer*
  » *The Workbook on Spiritual Disciplines*
  » *The Workbook on Abiding in Christ*
  » *The Workbook on Coping as Christians*
  » *The Workbook on the Beatitudes*
  » *The Workbook on Virtues and Fruits of the Spirit*

Encourage members to consider whether they may be called to recruit and lead a different group through this workbook. Many people are looking for a small group experience; there is always room for more groups, and that requires more leaders. The experience and excitement of those who have used the workbook will add credibility to their invitations to others.

Centering Prayer

Invite participants to center their spirits and hearts for this time of listening for God.

Opening Prayer

> LOVING GOD, WHO GAVE US JESUS *to save us and give us new life, we ask your blessing on our daily reading and reflection and on our sharing as a group. Calm our hearts and minds so we can hear clearly from you, from the Scripture, and from each other. Send your Spirit to guide us to love and respect each other as members of the body of Christ. We pray this in the name of our Teacher and Savior, Jesus Christ. Amen.*

Scripture Reading, followed by Silent Reflection

Read aloud the following Scripture passages; then have everyone reflect silently on the reading for about thirty seconds.

- Psalm 146:5-9, Isaiah 58:6-11, and Philippians 3:12-16

Prayer for Illumination

> GOD, QUIET OUR HEARTS that we may hear your voice. Grant us courage to follow your ways. Amen.

Bible Study

"Come to me, all you who are struggling hard and carrying heavy loads, and I will give you rest. Put on my yoke, and learn from me. I'm gentle and humble. And you will find rest for yourselves. My yoke is easy to bear, and my burden is light." (Matthew 11:28-30)

"I am the vine; you are the branches. If you remain in me and I in you, then you will produce much fruit. Without me, you can't do anything." (John 15:5)

Invite someone to read these passages aloud.

Discussion Question

On Day One, we looked at these passages as the "dual invitation" of Jesus. Have you personally responded to both invitations? Offer an example.

Discussion and Sharing

- Invite each person to share any new insight or learning received this week.
- On Day One, we looked at three ways that help us "constantly abide" in Christ: affirm and cultivate awareness of the indwelling Christ; practice a healthy dependence on Christ; identify things in ourselves that must die in order that we may

live and be alive in Christ. Have you engaged in any of these practices? If so, offer some examples, and describe how they affected your spiritual growth.
- In this workbook journey, we considered the explanation that justification is what God does *for* us and sanctification is what God does *in* us. Does that seem to be an accurate description? How have you seen this at work in your life?
- Using your own words, how would you explain *justification* and *sanctification* to someone?
- What does an intentional journey to "full salvation"—that is, being formed and living daily in Christ—entail in your life? How do you experience the indwelling Christ as the shaping power of your life? When was the last time you practiced what Christ has been and done in your life, and we must be and do for others?

Closing Prayer and Remarks

- If the group knows one of the doxologies in *The United Methodist Hymnal* (94 or 95), invite them to sing one together to begin your prayer time. Alternatively, sing a familiar chorus that expresses joy and thanksgiving. Some additional doxology options are listed in the index in the back of the *Hymnal*.
- For a closing time of corporate prayer, invite group members to share what they are most grateful for in their lives. Then invite them to share needs or concerns. When all have shared in this fashion, invite as many as will to offer brief prayers responding to both issues of gratitude and concern.
- Thank the group for their contributions to the discussion. Remind them of the time and location of the next meeting, if that varies from week to week.
- Remind them to pray for each other in the coming week.
- If a member is hosting the group in her or his home, ask the group to thank the host. Further, invite participants to clean up any papers, cups, or other items they may have left, and to help return the room to its original order, if that was changed for the meeting.

SESSION 8

GROWING ON TO SALVATION

Session Goals

This session will equip participants to

- understand the Wesleyan concept of sanctification; and
- adopt practices that help them "grow on to salvation."

Reading Assignments

Before this session, participants should have completed the eighth week of reading and reflection in *The Wesleyan Journey*.

Introduction for the Leader

This is the final meeting designed for this group. If the group has decided to continue meeting together, members should complete these plans.

Whatever they choose to do, determine the actual time line in advance so group members can make a clear commitment.

Assign some members to guide the group to follow through on its decision.

Centering Prayer

Invite participants to center their spirits and hearts for this time of listening for God.

Opening Prayer

> **LOVING GOD, WHO GAVE US JESUS** *to save us and give us new life, we ask your blessing on our daily reading and reflection and on our sharing as a group. Calm our hearts and minds so we can hear clearly from you, from the Scripture, and from each other. Send your Spirit to guide us to love and respect each other as members of the body of Christ. We pray this in the name of our Teacher and Savior, Jesus Christ. Amen.*

Scripture Reading, followed by Silent Reflection

Read aloud the following Scripture passages; then have everyone reflect silently on the reading for about thirty seconds.

- Psalm 25:4-15, Matthew 5:48, and Ephesians 5:1-2

Prayer for Illumination

> **FILL US FULL EVERY MORNING** *with your faithful love so we can rejoice and celebrate our whole life long (Psalm 90:14). May our hearts run over with your love as we share its abundance with others. Amen.*

Bible Study

Dear friends, let's love each other, because love is from God, and everyone who loves is born from God and knows God. The person who doesn't love does not know God, because God is love. This is how the love of God is revealed to us: God has sent his only Son into the world so that we can live through him. This is love: it is not that we loved God but that he loved us and sent his Son as the sacrifice that deals with our sins. (1 John 4:7-10)

Invite someone to read this passage aloud.

Discussion Question

How do others know that God's love is alive in you? Offer some examples.

Discussion and Sharing

Leader: Allow twenty to twenty-five minutes for the last discussion topic.

- What does this mean to you: "What Christ has been and done for us, we must seek to be and do for others"?
- Spend eight to ten minutes discussing the claim that we must allow the working power of God in the past to be brought into the present. How would you do that in your own life?
- Discuss how "acting as a Christian" is a means of grace. Has this been a part of your awareness? How have you experienced this?
- Invite someone to read aloud the last two paragraphs of the reading for Day Five. If every Christian is called to be a servant, how might you need to change your style of serving if it is to be like that of Jesus?
- Spend eight to ten minutes discussing the meaning of holiness and sanctification:
  » What does it mean?
  » Where are you in your sanctification?
  » What might help you take the call to holiness seriously?
- What have these eight weeks in this group meant to you? Do you have new insights and learnings, challenges, or issues you wish to work on? What will help you to do that?

Closing Prayer and Remarks

- Join hands and sing a familiar hymn or chorus. Then invite participants to offer brief sentence prayers of thanksgiving and intercession for one another.
- Thank the group for their contributions to the discussion. If they have decided to continue meeting, review the next steps they have agreed upon.
- Remind them to pray for each other in the coming week.
- If a member is hosting the group in her or his home, ask the group to thank the host. Further, invite participants to clean up any papers, cups, or other items they may have left, and to help return the room to its original order, if that was changed for the meeting.